INTRODUCTION

Norwich is rich in bridges and they are of great architectural and historical interest. Yet they seem to attract little attention, 'harmless and necessary', like Shakespeare's cat, and perpetually in need of repair, but not highly regarded. Two 13th century men were however sufficiently fond of their bridges to remember them in their wills: John Bond left 6d to Fifbridge, and in 1272 William de Dunwich left 2s each to St Martins and Newbridge (Whitefriars and St George's).

By 1300 there were five bridges over the Wensum in Norwich, more than any other city in England, including London. These were Bishop, Whitefriars, Fye, St George's and St Miles Coslany. It was also possible to cross the Yare to the south of Norwich at Trowse, Harford, Earlham and Cringleford, a very large number of bridges in a comparatively small area. The reason lies in Norwich's great importance as a commercial, administrative and religious centre, which originated in Saxon times, and was consolidated by the Normans. Bridges were necessary to link the various settlements on both sides of the river, and for trade and communications. The exact origins of these bridges are shrouded in obscurity, which seems surprising, as it must have been an enormous advantage to cross by a bridge, rather than wait for a ferry or use a muddy ford.

With the exception of Bishop Bridge these early bridges were built of wood and required much upkeep: the tolls imposed on all passengers were intended for maintenance, and there are numerous references to decay and repair in the history books. Houses at this time were 'not the quasi-permanent objects of later centuries, but consumer durables, something to be replaced every so often', so perhaps bridges were seen in the same light.

Norwich's prosperity continued, and during the 16th century there was much building activity of a more permanent nature. New Mills was renovated, Fye, St Miles, St George's and Whitefriars were rebuilt in stone, and Hellesdon Bridge was taken over by the City. It is thought the physical appearance of Norwich changed little after this time until the mid 18th century, and even in 1800 many medieval features still existed, including bridges which were 'old, narrow and humpbacked.' St George's, built in stone in 1784, was the outstanding exception.

At the beginning of the 19th century there was an increasing awareness that action needed to be taken to modernise Norwich. In 1805 the City applied for an 'Act for the Better Paving, Lighting, Cleansing, Watching and otherwise Improving the City of Norwich', and the following year a Board of Improvement Commissioners was set up. This commission was instrumental in rebuilding St Miles Coslany, Hellesdon and Fye bridges, and for constructing new bridges at Carrow and Foundry; all apart from the latter were built of iron. Recession in the middle of the century meant that little more was done, but the railways, which East Anglia was slow to develop, brought fresh impetus to trade and helped to restore prosperity. The present-day Foundry bridge, the 1882 City Station bridge and the two A frame rail bridges, also built in iron, all owe their existence to the railways.

This process of expansion and modernisation has continued through the 20th century, though concrete is now the building material.

Norwich is fortunate in having such a variety of bridges and it is hoped that this book will stimulate greater interest in them. The best way to appreciate the present-day bridges is to use the river walk which stretches, with minor interruptions, from Carrow to Hellesdon Mill.

CARROW BRIDGE

The first bridge at Carrow was not on the present site, but 175 yards downstream: the road ran down Carrow Hill, through what is now Colman's factory, across the river and straight into Carrow Road. It was a fixed bridge, as can be seen from the contemporary painting, and it is interesting to note how rural the area was at that time. There was much opposition to the idea of a bridge here from the supporters of the proposed rival Foundry Bridge. In the early 19th century all bridges still charged a toll, and there was not thought to be sufficient traffic to support two bridges. Nevertheless, Carrow went ahead and Thomas Back, mayor of Norwich, laid the first stone on 6 August 1810.

In the 1830s the City Council had plans to promote Norwich as a port for sea-going ships, to reduce its dependence on Great Yarmouth and to cut out the pilfering which occurred when goods were trans-shipped into wherries. The fixed bridge was replaced in 1833 by a double bascule lifting bridge which was more practical, though not so picturesque.

The increase in road and river traffic by the end of the century meant that a new bridge was needed, but plans for a replacement were delayed by difficulties over the site and by the First World War. After the war there were long and complex negotiations between Colman's, the Great Eastern Railway and the City. As a result the site for the new bridge was moved upstream, because of pressure from Colman's, who did not want their factory divided by a public road. The City also hoped for a grant from the Ministry of Transport, which they believed depended on providing a better road link along Riverside Road.

Work was finally started in 1920 as part of an unemployment relief scheme. Colman's contributed £10,000 and Boulton and Paul £5,000 towards the total cost of £42,000. The bridge was designed by the City Engineer, A E Collins, and is a single leaf bascule bridge. It was opened with considerable pomp on 27 June 1923 (the year that the Norwich Society was founded) by the Prince of Wales, the future Edward VIII.

There was a lot of commercial traffic on the river up until the 1950s, but nowadays the warehouses are empty or converted to other uses and the bridge is seldom lifted. The mechanism is much affected by the temperature: during the winter of 1962/3 it took 12 minutes 20 seconds to lift, rather than the normal 3 minutes, and on one occasion in the very hot summer of 1976 it refused to lift until 8pm, despite repeated hosings.

The remains of the two boom towers that were built in the 14th century by Richard Spynk can be seen next to the present bridge. Chains or booms used to be stretched across the river at night to prevent marauders from invading the city, and vessels from leaving without paying their dues. At one time the tower on the east side of the river was used as a prison.

Left:
The first Carrow Bridge built 1810
Watercolour by an unknown artist

Left:
Second Carrow Bridge built 1833

Below:
Carrow Bridge built 1923

FOUNDRY BRIDGE

Until 1811 there was no bridge on this site but by this time Thorpe had grown in importance and it was considered necessary to connect it to the centre. The City appealed to Parliament for an act to construct a bridge over the the Wensum at or near the Foundry.

The first stone of Foundry Bridge was laid by Alderman J Davey on 6 August 1810 and it was opened the following year. It was mainly built of timber with Portland stone abutments and cast iron railings: there was very little room for boats to pass underneath. It seems that neither this bridge nor the first one at Carrow were built with much concern for river traffic.

The Foundry stood a little downstream from the Hotel Nelson, and its tall chimney can be seen in old prints. Iron founding was one of the less well-known but important industries in Norwich at this time, there being great demand for cast iron items for both domestic and industrial purposes.

Thorpe Station was opened in 1844 with a rail link to Great Yarmouth. This meant a large increase in traffic and a new larger bridge, described as 'a little bridge by the Foundry', was opened the same year. The railway company contributed £2000, half the cost, and the rest was paid out of the dues that were still levied on all goods arriving in Norwich by river.

Norwich in 1800 was one of the country's wealthiest cities, chiefly because of the worsted trade. This suffered a decline in the 1830s and it was not until later in the century that new industries were established to replace it. Renewed prosperity brought demands for better communications. Rose Lane was narrow, winding and congested, and a new road, Prince of Wales Road, was built in 1862. It was built to low standards by private enterprise, and in 1865 was taken over by the City, which had to reconstruct it two years later as it was 'much cut up in trenches and greatly in need of repair.' The City wall at Chapel Field was being demolished at this time and the rubble was used as foundations for the road.

By the 1870s, there was again pressure to replace the bridge owing to increasing industrial and residential development. The Norwich Improvement Act was passed in 1879, and work started in September 1884. The new bridge was 50 ft wide, 5 ft wider than intended: this was fortunate, given modern traffic flows. The Great Eastern Railway, which opened the present Thorpe Station in 1886, contributed 10% to the total cost of £12,000.

This busy junction could have been worse: the Eastern Daily Press reported in 1969 that plans existed for a two level crossing 'which only requires government financial approval' - this fortunately was not forthcoming.

Right:
The first Foundry Bridge built 1811

Watercolour by J J Cotman

Inset: Spout for fire brigade hose

Below:
The second Foundry Bridge built 1844
Lithograph by an unknown artist

Bottom : Foundry Bridge Today

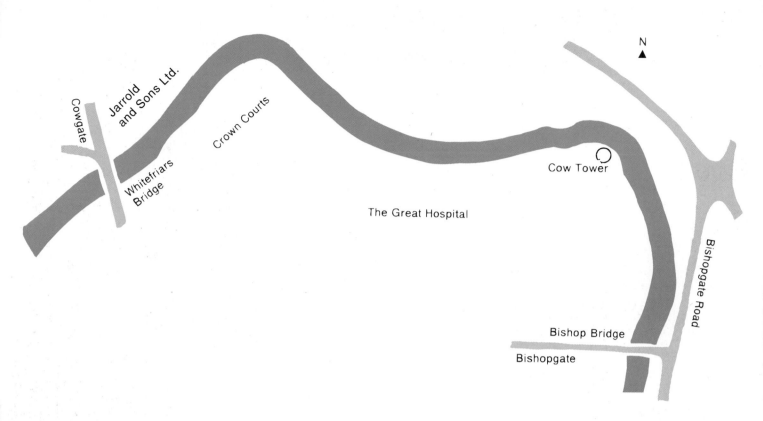

BISHOP BRIDGE

This is the only surviving medieval bridge in Norwich, and reputed to be the oldest one in the country still in daily use. There is mention of a bridge being repaired by the Bishop in 1249, and in 1275 a patent was granted to William de Kerkeby to build a gate with a bridge adjoining.

The present bridge was built by Richard Spynk between 1337 and 1341. It was the first in Norwich to be built of stone, and originally had a large gatehouse on the western end, since the bridge formed part of the City's defences. The gatehouse can be seen in the painting by Alfred Stannard, which was based on a much earlier engraving.

The bridge originally belonged to the church, but since 1393, as Blomefield said: 'it hath belonged to and been maintained by the City. They always appointed a porter to live over and keep the gates, but the hermit which dwelt by them was always nominated by the prior and the hermit's house at the Dissolution passed to the church.'

During Kett's Rebellion the bridge and gatehouse were damaged when the rebels, encamped on Mousehold Heath, tried to enter Norwich. Nicholas Sotherton's contemporary account of the rebellion states that when Kett was trying to capture the City he sent 'vagabond boys, naked and unarmed', across the river. They ran among the enemy archers and seized arrows to return to their own side. They even plucked arrows from their bodies and legs and handed them, still dripping with blood, to the rebel archers who fired them at the enemy.

A survey carried out in 1790 found that the weight of the gatehouse was causing great cracks to open in the arches, and that the whole building leant to the north. It was recommended that the structure be taken down to save the bridge and this was done the following year.

In 1923 the City wanted to widen Bishop Bridge, which would have meant its destruction. A group of concerned citizens formed the Norwich Society to oppose the plan. Over the past 71 years the Society has campaigned actively to save buildings and areas of outstanding interest and to encourage high standards in new developments.

Recently there has been increasing concern about the amount of traffic using the bridge and it may have to be closed to traffic to ensure its survival.

Above: Bishop Bridge. Drawing by Robert Dixon 1810

Right: Two of the stone heads which can be seen under the arches

Below: Bishop Bridge today

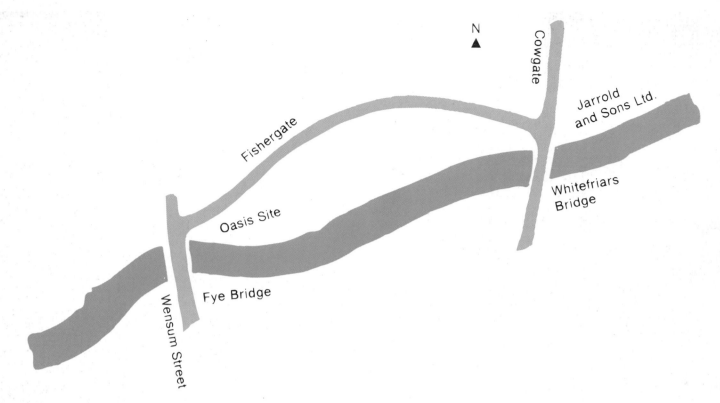

WHITEFRIARS BRIDGE

Whitefriars is the earliest recorded bridge in Norwich. According to Hudson it dates from 1106, and he comments: 'a line of communication important enough to lead to the building of a bridge must have existed at St Martin's (the old name for Whitefriars) before Fyebridge was built.' It derives its name from the Carmelite or White Friars who came to Norwich in 1256 and built an extensive Priory here which lasted until the Dissolution. An undercroft and the remains of an anchorite cell can still be seen and now form part of Jarrold's print museum.

There is little mention of this bridge during the medieval period except in 1289/90 when it was flooded. It was rebuilt several times, always in wood.

During Kett's Rebellion in 1549 it was demolished by the Earl of Warwick to prevent the rebels from entering Norwich. After the rebellion it was rebuilt, and 'Mr Codde the mayor contributed much' to the cost. Once again, it was a wooden bridge with three narrow arches which impeded the flow of the water. In 1591 it was replaced by a 30ft, single span, stone bridge decorated with battlements and two turrets. The turrets lasted until the reign of James I and the battlements were replaced in 1835 with neat iron railings when the bridge was refurbished. Other than this there were no changes until the bridge was demolished in 1924.

The river was very narrow at this point and therefore prone to flooding. To alleviate the problem, the City decided to widen the river, which meant removing the bridge. The Norwich Society campaigned hard to save it, but was defeated. As a compromise, it was agreed to preserve the old stones, which were carefully taken down and numbered. They mysteriously disappeared: some accounts say they were used for constructing the new Aylsham Road, others that they were taken by river to Wroxham to be used as foundations for bungalows. In either case, it was an ignominious end for such an old and pretty bridge.

The present bridge was designed by A E Collins, the City Engineer. It was constructed in 1924/5 as part of a scheme to alleviate unemployment.

The old Silk Yarn Mills, now Jarrold Printing, can be seen from this point. Designed by John Brown and built in 1836-9, it was the first steam powered factory in Norwich. It is now considered to be one of the country's finest examples of early Victorian industrial architecture.

Above: photograph of Whitefriars Bridge in 1886

Below: present Whitefriars Bridge

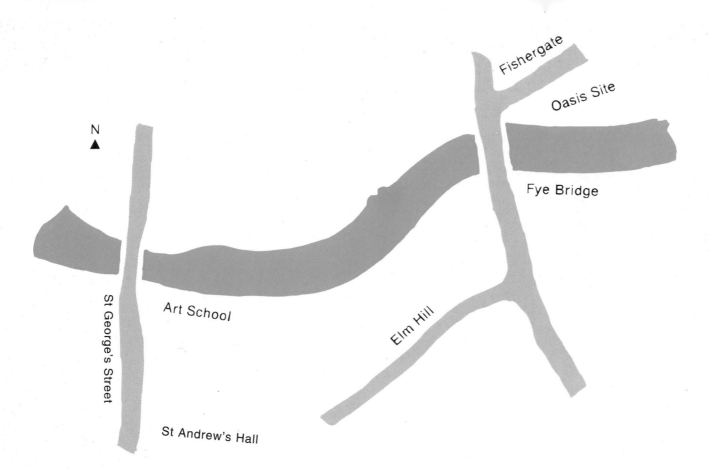

FYE BRIDGE

Fye Bridge is first mentioned in 1132 and thus vies with Whitefriars for the title of earliest bridge over the Wensum. Old maps show that it does provide a link between King Street, one of the oldest streets in Norwich, and Magdalen Street, the main northern route out of the city. Blomefield, however, says : 'Fyvebridge, as it is anciently called, took its name on account of being the fifth bridge over the river at this time.'

In 1283 the City made an agreement with Walter de Monton for 'the sustentation of the bridge so that passengers may have free and convenient passage. Walter may construct at his will sheds on the bridge', and by 1346 there were shops here as well.

Blomefield continues; 'It was a timber bridge until Henry IV's time, and it was then built of stone with two arches, being the first stone bridge that was in this place. It fell into decay in Henry V's time and was broken down by a great flood in 1570, and was new built of stone in 1573 and it hath over it this inscription:

1572 Robert Suckling Mayor 1573 Mr Thomas Pack Mayor

Peter Peterson Chamberlaine'

The customs on this bridge went to maintain it, and it lasted until 1829 when it was replaced by a new bridge, designed by Francis Stone. It was reconstructed in the 1930s, to provide work for the unemployed. The work took from August 1931 to May 1934 to complete, much to the annoyance of the traders in Magdalen Street.

There is a plaque on the bridge which commemorates the existence in the sixteenth century of a 'Ducking Stool where common skoulds and disreputable characters could receive the cold water cure.' It is also reputed to be a place where witches were drowned.

On a more cheerful note, the Oasis, a piece of waste ground by the bridge between Fishergate and the river, was tidied up by the Norwich Society for public enjoyment. It was opened by the Duke of Edinburgh in 1975 as part of Norwich's award winning entry for European Architectural Heritage Year.

Above: Fye Bridge. Watercolour by John Thirtle 1807

Below: present Fye Bridge reconstructed in 1934

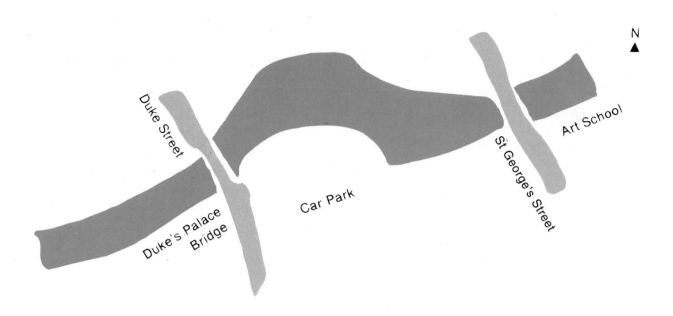

ST GEORGE'S BRIDGE

The present bridge was described in 1961 in the Eastern Evening News as 'another inconvenient survivor from another age.' It could more accurately be called the most aristocratic bridge in Norwich, having been designed by Sir John Soane, the architect of the Bank of England, and creator of the Soane House Museum in London. It was built in 1784 of Portland stone and has a single span of 42 ft. It was originally designed to have two stone staircases at each end on the downstream side. Only one was built but now no longer exists. There was no room for the other one 'on account of the houses being too near on that side.' There are two niches on the same side, but statues were never installed.

The original bridge was known as New Bridge, which would imply that it was the most recent of the five medieval crossings over the Wensum. Like the others it was periodically rebuilt in timber and eventually, in the sixteenth century, in stone. This lasted until 1784 when the present bridge was built.

In 1930 the City wanted to widen St George's Street and the bridge was therefore threatened, but the Norwich Society campaigned hard to save it and in this case was successful.

The Dominicans or Black Friars, after whom the bridge derives one of its names, originally came to Norwich in the 13th century and settled in a street which later became known as Black Boys Lane, after the colour of their robes. They had a great effect upon Norwich; they chose to settle in poor districts and as they were very good preachers, they were responsible for a surge of religious enthusiasm. The priory buildings were extensive, as can be judged from St Andrews and Blackfriars Halls, the nave and choir of the old church.

Nowadays the Art School, (now known as the Norfolk Institute of Art & Design) another building designed by A E Collins, dominates the site, and interrupts the river walk. Its dark north wall drops sheer into the water, a feature taken advantage of by past (and perhaps present) art students wishing to dispose of misshapen plaster casts which fell into the Wensum with a satisfying plop.

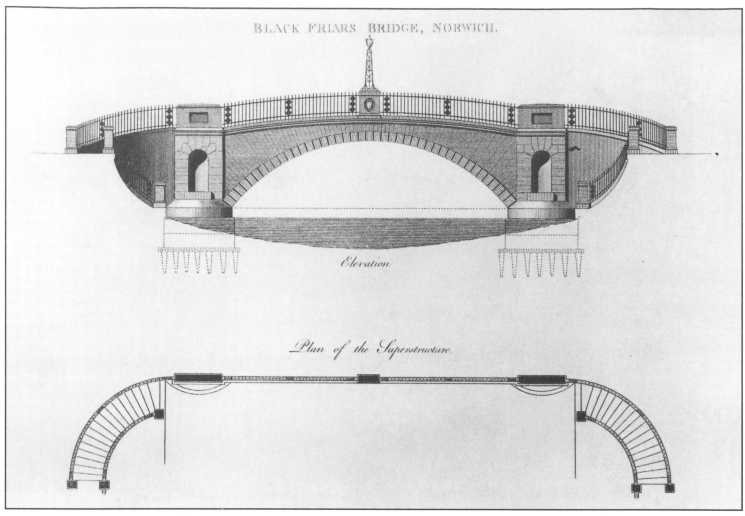

Above: Architect's Elevation and Plan of Blackfriars Bridge, now called St George's

Below: St George's Bridge today

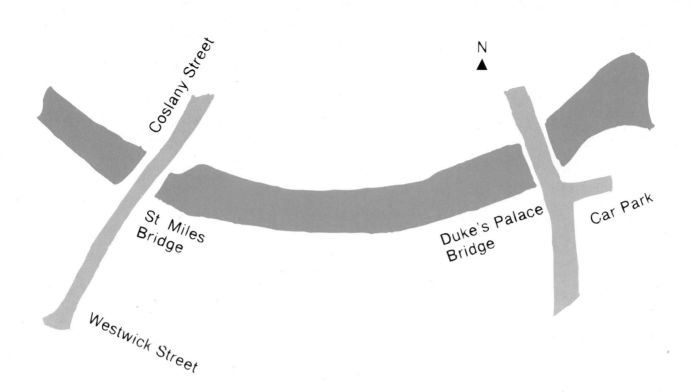

DUKE'S PALACE BRIDGE

Duke's Palace Bridge is one of the more modern crossings: the first bridge dates from 1822. Before that, ferries were the only means of crossing the river between St Miles Coslany and Blackfriars, which meant that a large part of Norwich known as 'over the water' was cut off from the centre.

An action committee was formed to press for the building of a bridge which encountered a great deal of local opposition. Eventually the necessary act of parliament was passed, and the first stone was laid on 28 August 1821. Designed by Henry Lock, and cast by John Brown of Norwich, it was hailed as a masterpiece, with its 60ft elliptical arch and pierced balustrading. It is the last bridge to span the Wensum within the City walls. A toll of 1/2d for foot passengers was imposed to pay for the construction; this practice continued until 1855, when the bridge was purchased by the City for £4000 and the toll abolished. A special dinner was held to celebrate the event.

When Duke Street was widened in 1972 the bridge was demolished, and the City decided to sell the cast iron arches for scrap for £400. The Norwich Society stepped in and bought them. and stored them for many years. They were given to the Castle Mall development in 1992. The best parts of each were restored and combined into one arch which can now be seen over the car park entrance in Rose Avenue.

The old Duke's Palace was on the site of the present multi-storey car park and the telephone exchange (what a falling off was there). Built by Henry Howard 6th Duke of Norfolk, it was partially destroyed in 1711, but the banqueting hall with its heavily decorated barrel ceiling remained in use as a billiard room until after the second world war.

The Art School can be seen in the distance, as can the Cathedral spire.

Above:
Duke's Palace Bridge

Unfinished watercolour by John Thirtle c 1822

Left:
Present Duke's Palace Bridge built 1972

Below:
Old Duke's Palace Bridge forming entrance to car park at Castle Mall

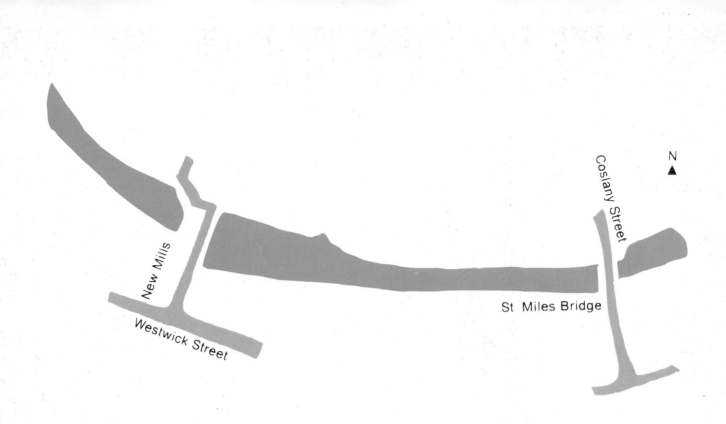

ST MILES COSLANY BRIDGE

Very little is known about the first bridge here, but undoubtedly this is the site of a very early crossing. There were originally two bridges between a central island. The name Coslany is reputed to be Anglo-Saxon for 'island in a bog.'

In 1521 a stone bridge replaced the earlier wooden one as part of a general rebuilding in Norwich. The local saying 'When dragon drinks, Heigham sinks' referred to the dragon carved on the keystone. There were bad floods at intervals throughout Norwich's history, the worst being in August 1912, and several bridges have plaques recording the water levels.

The present bridge, which dates from 1804, is the earliest iron bridge in Norwich and one of the most attractive. It was designed by James Frost who was also responsible for Hellesdon bridge 15 years later. The design includes a spout for the fire brigade hoses, similar to the ones on Foundry and Duke's Palace Bridge.

In medieval times this area was an important centre for the dyeing industry. Until recently there was much industrial activity and the bridge was an important link to Norwich 'over the water'. With the industry gone and the bridge closed to traffic it is now a quiet and pleasant residential area, with part of the old Anchor Brewery acting as the centrepiece.

St Lawrence's church can be seen from Coslany Street. Built in the 15th century, it replaced an earlier church mentioned in the Domesday book.

St Miles Bridge built 1804

NEW MILLS

'There were iv auncenne mylles here ever since the Conquest and before', according to a 15th century document. The mills stood on the bank of the Wensum a little way upstream from the present bridge and were the Appleyard, Bumpstead mills and the two Calke-Mills. Like Hellesdon Mills they were both corn and fulling mills.

In 1401-2, a surveyor called Blaumester was bought from Colchester at the cost of 6/8d to 'examine the place for the water mills to be new built'. The mills however were only completed 28 years later, when an official miller was put in charge of them. All city bakers were expected to grind their corn here and could be fined for not doing so.

All was well for ten years, but in 1440 the Abbot of St Benet's decided to prosecute the City: he said the new mills stopped the water, making it overflow the banks and damage his land in Heigham. He also claimed that he had right of passage: 'he and his predecessors might rowe with his botes from his mills and manor onto the heye see without tyme of mynde of man.' The City retorted that the Abbot's own mills stopped the water, the river had not been navigable since 1250 and further that the 'old mills stood long decayed and it were a great desolacion if the people had not the new mills.'

As Stacey explains, 'the dispute ended in a riot called Gladman's Insurrection, from John Gladman, merchant, who rode on horseback as a King, with a paper crown on, and a sceptre and sword carried before him. At this rebellion Wetherby, the ally of the Abbot, pulled up the flood gates of the new mills and destroyed them, so that the bakers were forced to seek for mills ten miles around, to the great hurt and damage of the City during all these years the mills stood so decayed.'

In the reign of Queen Elizabeth I, water works were started here and in 1582 water was pumped to the Market Cross. By 1800 there was an 'intermittent, unfiltered, and impure' water supply for those who were able and willing to pay for it.

In the 19th century, Norwich was extremely unhygienic, and the Wensum was 'thoroughly and irremediably' polluted with domestic and industrial waste of every description: there were 120 sewers between Carrow and New Mills. New waterworks were opened in 1869 but the sewage system took longer to improve and it was not until 1898 that the New Mills Pumping Station was built. This provided compressed air for pumping sewage, using the Shone ejector system. The turbines were worked by the tides, with a back-up system when the tides were insufficient.

A survey carried out in 1936, when the sewerage was extended, found that the system was still in good working order, a tribute to the materials and workmanship of the Victorians.

The pumping station was closed in 1974 and the building is currently being restored, with the intention of creating an Industrial Museum. The sluices are still in operation and used to control the water level.

N

City Station Bridges

Station Road

New Mills

Above: New Mills Oil painting by John Crome c 1815

Below: New Mills today

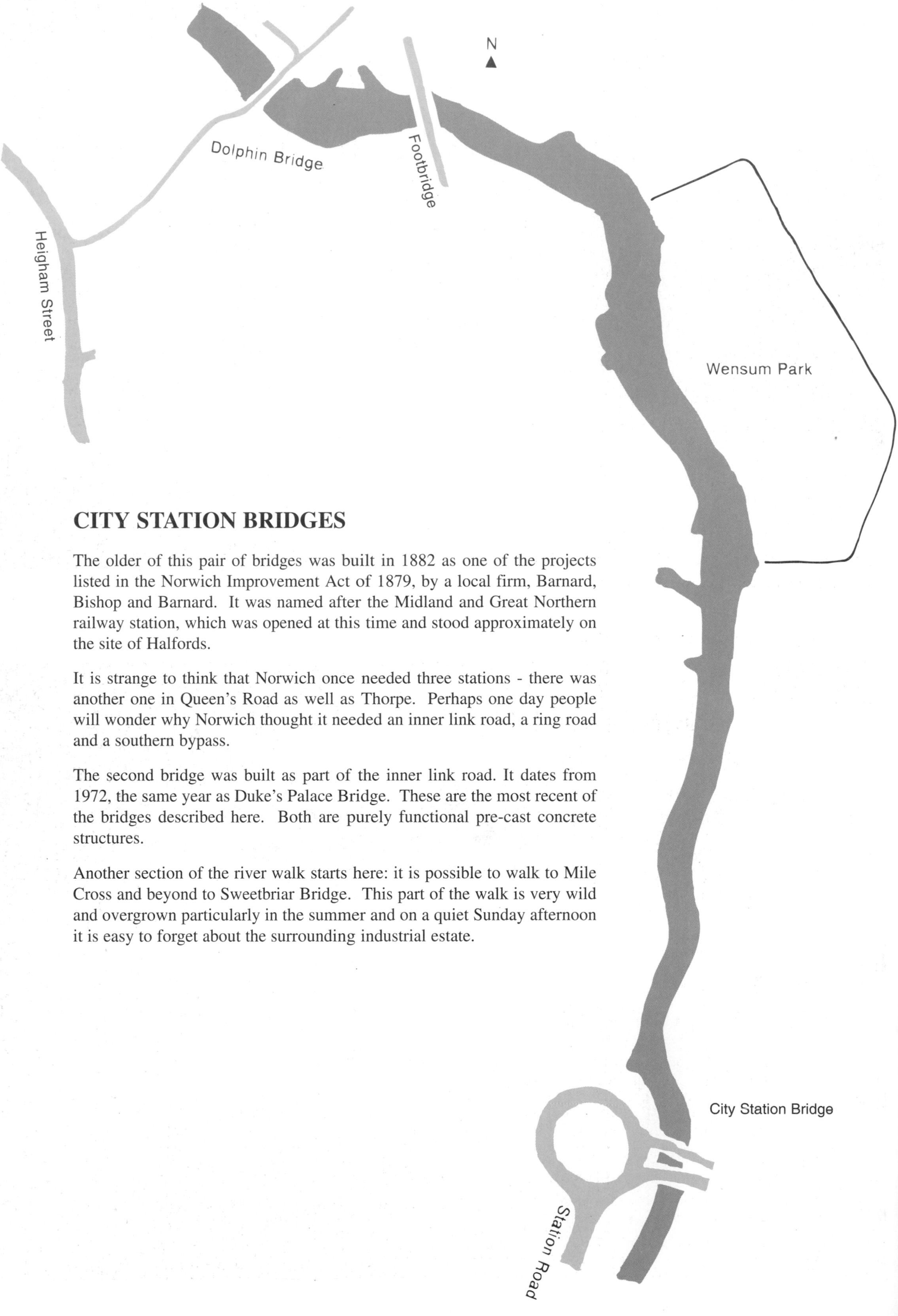

Dolphin Bridge

Footbridge

N
▲

Heigham Street

Wensum Park

CITY STATION BRIDGES

The older of this pair of bridges was built in 1882 as one of the projects listed in the Norwich Improvement Act of 1879, by a local firm, Barnard, Bishop and Barnard. It was named after the Midland and Great Northern railway station, which was opened at this time and stood approximately on the site of Halfords.

It is strange to think that Norwich once needed three stations - there was another one in Queen's Road as well as Thorpe. Perhaps one day people will wonder why Norwich thought it needed an inner link road, a ring road and a southern bypass.

The second bridge was built as part of the inner link road. It dates from 1972, the same year as Duke's Palace Bridge. These are the most recent of the bridges described here. Both are purely functional pre-cast concrete structures.

Another section of the river walk starts here: it is possible to walk to Mile Cross and beyond to Sweetbriar Bridge. This part of the walk is very wild and overgrown particularly in the summer and on a quiet Sunday afternoon it is easy to forget about the surrounding industrial estate.

City Station Bridge

Station Road

Above: New pre-cast concrete bridge built 1972

Below: Original cast iron bridge built 1882

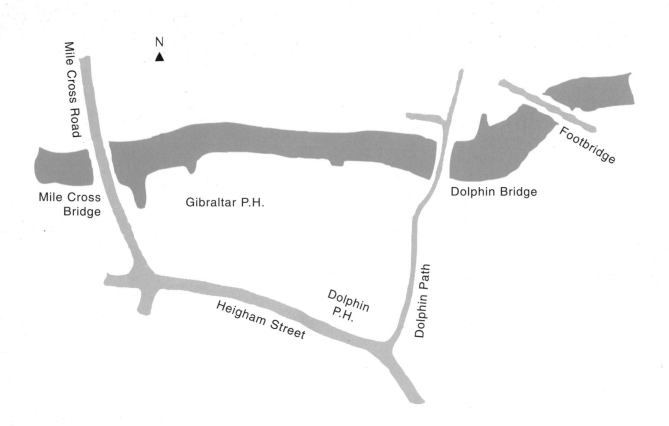

DOLPHIN BRIDGE

There were several old ferries here, notably Piggin's Ferry. At one time there was an island called Four Tree Island. The trees fell one by one and eventually the island disappeared.

The expansion of Norwich in the early part of the 20th century meant that there was great demand for a crossing at this point. When the footbridge opened in 1909, many people thought it should have been a road bridge. It is a very substantial reinforced concrete bridge and an early example of this type of construction. Originally there was an extension over the railway line, and although built in the same material, it was a complete contrast, being a much lighter and more advanced form of concrete construction. This part was taken down after the railway closed.

The footpath leads to the Dolphin Inn. Bishop Hall retired here after he had been ousted from the Bishop's Palace by the Puritans; he died in the house on 8 September 1656 and was buried in the nearby church of St Bartholomew. The house is dated 1587 on the lintel over the door and 1610 in the flintwork, but it was badly damaged in the air-raids of 1942 and was reconstructed after the war in the original style.

The old Eagle Swimming Baths were situated here. Boys and girls were segregated, unless they were brave enough to swim in the muddy and reed-lined river.

A little further downstream there was an A frame railway bridge very similar to the one still existing at Hellesdon. It was taken down and replaced in 1986 with a wooden footbridge, though the old abutments were retained.

Above: Footbridge built in 1986 on the abutments of the old rail bridge

Below: the Dolphin footbridge built 1909

Sweetbriar Road

Sweetbriar Road Bridge

MILE CROSS BRIDGE

This concrete bridge was completed in 1923 together with Mile Cross Road. It was part of an unemployment relief scheme and 90% of the workforce were ex-service men. In 1921 the project was visited by King George V and Queen Mary.

The total cost of the road and bridge was £47,000, which was justified by the director-general of roads at the Ministry of Transport in his opening speech: 'These new roads and bridges are an essential necessity. If during this period of depression, we can put such works in hand with beneficial results to the trade of the country, then surely we should be most unwise to see our citizens unwillingly idle and compelled to seek doles and charity with the corollary of loss of dignity and independence which such forms of maintenance are bound to bring in their train.'

It was realised that concrete was the building material of the future and another benefit of the scheme was that it provided a workforce trained in new skills.

One drawback of this road-building was that one wing of the old Dial House was destroyed, despite pressure from the Norwich Society. Ironically, the destroyed wing included the sun-dial. The Dial House has belonged to the City for many years, and has been shamefully neglected. At the time of writing, it is up for sale to be converted into offices.

The old name of this site was Heigham Watering, because it was here that cattle stopped for a drink on their way to the Norwich Cattle Market while their drovers visited the Gibraltar Gardens.

This ancient practice continued until the new road and bridge were built.

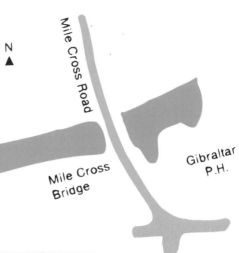

N ▲

Mile Cross Road

Mile Cross Bridge

Gibraltar P.H.

Right: Mile Cross Bridge built 1923

Below: Mile Cross Bridge from Anderson's Meadow

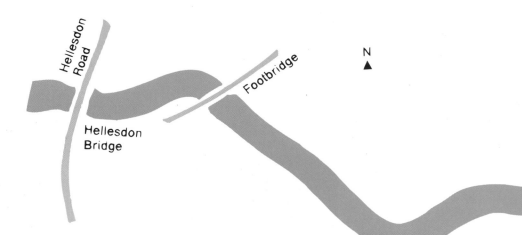

SWEETBRIAR BRIDGE

It is easy to overlook Sweetbriar Bridge while driving along the A47, but, seen from the allotments on the upstream side, it is quite a handsome concrete structure, built in the 1930s when the area was chosen for industrial development and the ring road was built. Sweetbriar Lane was until then a quiet country road. Only one letter to the press protested against its destruction.

Like Mile Cross, it was built to alleviate unemployment and to train a new workforce in the use of reinforced concrete. Although it is a modern structure, it does have features that echo the past.

The river walk is interrupted by the allotments and the gardens of the Gate House pub although a continuous walk was originally intended. Once past the pub, it is a very pleasant rural walk all the way to Hellesdon Mill.

Sweetbriar Bridge winter

Sweetbriar Bridge from the allotments

Sweetbriar Road

Sweetbriar
Road Bridge

Sweetbriar Bridge summer

HELLESDON BRIDGE

Since 1556 'the outward bank of the river by Hellesdon Bridge and from there to the old mill dam' has been part of the City and the City was responsible for its upkeep. In 1621 the bridge was described as 'ruinated and decayed and dangerous for people wanting to use it', and a new timber bridge was built.

Floods caused by a rapid thaw after a great snowfall badly damaged it in 1673 and in 1690 a committee was set up to supervise repairs. The present iron bridge, designed by James Frost, was built at a cost of £1,169 in 1819. Two plaques under the bridge instruct passing boats to keep to starboard. It is very narrow and a footbridge was recently added which obscures the view of the bridge from the downstream side.

The Midland and Great Northern Railway which linked Norwich to Cromer, Sheringham, King's Lynn and the Midlands built an A Frame bridge here in 1882. It is a little downstream from the road bridge and now carries a footpath. Although rather crude and dilapidated, it seems quite romantic when seen from a distance through summer vegetation.

Sir John Falstof acquired the Manor of Hellesdon in 1432, and lived here for many years. He has no connection with Shakespeare's Falstaff, and there was much indignation in the 17th century that Shakespeare was 'making an ignorant shift of abusing Sir John Falstof, by making him a Thrasonical puff and emblem of mock valour.'

When Sir John Falstof died he left his Hellesdon estates to his manager John Paston of the letters. The will was bitterly contested, as it was not thought appropriate for a mere manager to inherit such an estate and this legacy was to cause the Pastons a lot of trouble over a number of years.

William Yelverton, described by Margaret Paston as a 'good thredbare friend', challenged the will: he and his allies succeeded in having John Paston outlawed and by 1465 he was imprisoned in the Fleet Prison in London.

Margaret relates 'many trobelows matters' in her letters to her husband: their tenants' cattle were seized and they were continually harassed so that 'they be dayly in fear of ther lyves.'

Eventually 300 of the Duck - as she calls him - of Suffolk's men came to Hellesdon but the 'garyson' was forewarned and well prepared and managed to repel them. Later that year they returned and destroyed the house and ransacked the church, terrorising the Paston tenants into helping them to break down the walls. Margaret wrote to her husband: 'Ther will no cryatur thynke how fowle and orubelly it is arayed but yf they see it. There cometh much pepyll daily to wonder ther uppon, both of Norwich and other places.'

Finally, in 1478, while John Paston, grandson of the original John, was in London trying to assert his claim to the estate, the Duke of Suffolk took the Hellesdon estate over without any opposition.

River Tud

Old Malt House and Granary Buildings

Hellesdon Mills

N

Hellesdon Bridge

Hellesdon Road

Footbridge

Above: old Railway Bridge, now a footbridge

Below: Hellesdon Bridge built 1819

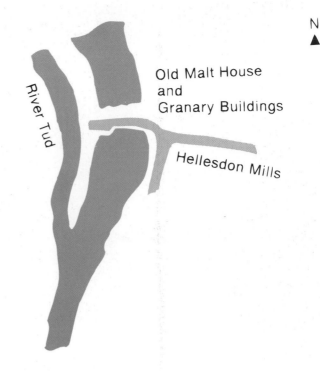

HELLESDON MILLS

It has probably been possible to cross the river here since Anglo-Saxon times, and by the time of the Domesday book, there were two mills. Margaret Paston refers to one of them, in a letter to her husband John, as being let, with the miller being asked to 'fynde the reparacion.'

Some time after this, the mills were abandoned and fell into decay. The 1556 document incorporating Hellesdon Mills into the city boundary refers to the 'old mille damme of the late water mill' at Hellesdon.

Kenneth Hipper says: 'these early mills were fulling mills - this meant that apart from grinding corn they were used to carry out the fulling process necessary in the manufacture of woollen goods. Cloth straight from the loom was washed and cleansed of dirt and grease. This process thickened the fibres and induced them to felt.'

He continues: 'Hellesdon was without a water mill for about 200 years, then in 1683 William Gostlin of Woolverstone Park in Suffolk leased an estate in Hellesdon and sought permission to build a mill at Hellesdon. At first the Bishop was reluctant to give permission because he thought that a mill at Hellesdon would hinder the Norwich mills.'

Eventually permission was granted and the mill was opened in 1684. It stood on the same site as the old mills and was built largely of wood. In 1719 the mill was extensively restored, and a new mill house was built, but in 1805 it was almost totally destroyed by fire. It was rebuilt and William Wells purchased it in 1848. Kenneth Hipper describes the work Wells undertook: 'he reconstructed and refitted the mill and mill house. In addition he had erected dwelling houses, cottages, warehouses, stables, drying kilns, blacksmith's and carpenter's shops, offices and other buildings for the purpose of his business as miller. Hellesdon mill was now one of the most impressive mills in Norfolk. The mill was four storeys high and set in the south side were 66 windows. There were four waterways beneath it.'

'The mill was pulled down in 1920 and the timber was used for housing at the Angel Estate. Today all that remains of the mill are the brick foundations with the four waterways and a small part of the eastern end of the mill.' The malthouse and granary buildings still exist, but are now used as a furniture store.

Above: Hellesdon Mill after 1851 reconstruction

Below: Hellesdon Mill today
One of the old millstones can be seen in the foreground

BIBLIOGRAPHY

James Campbell
Historic Towns: Norwich - The Scolar Press/
The Historic Towns Trust

Barbara Green & Rachel Young
Norwich, the Growth of a City - Norfolk Museums Service

Christopher Barringer Ed
Norwich in the 19th century - Gliddon Books

Kenneth Hipper
A History of Hellesdon Village

R S Joby
Hellesdon Past & Present - Klofron

F Blomefield
History of Norfolk

George Nobbs and Hamilton Wood
Davenport's Norwich

W Hudson and J C Tingey
Records of the City of Norwich

Eastern Daily Press
Eastern Evening News

Sir Sidney Lee
Life of Shakespeare

City of Norwich Amenities
The Norwich Blackfriars - a History and Guide to the Friary

The Paston Letters Vol II

Rachel Young

Norwich Discovery Walks

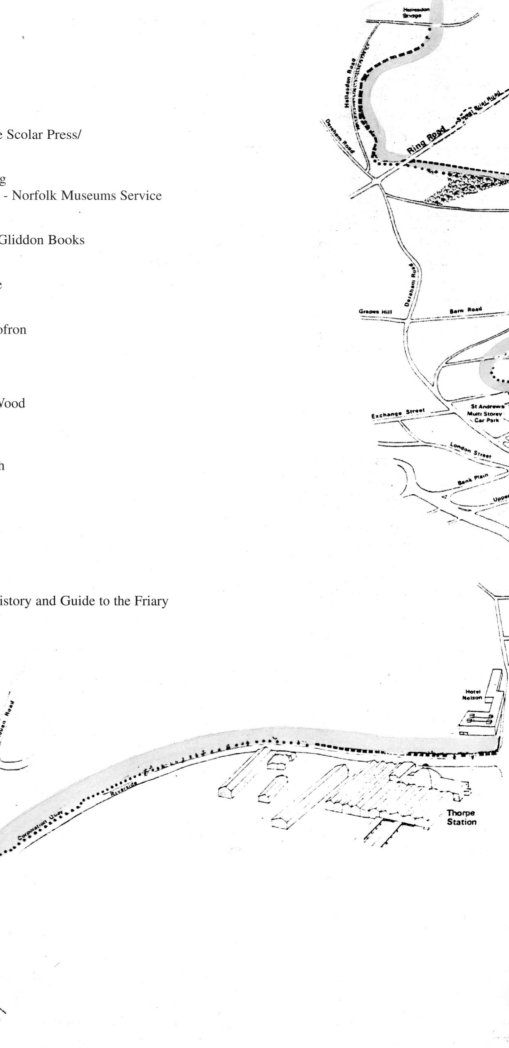